Big Honkin' Zits

A Zits® Treasury

by JERRY SCOTT and JIM BORGMAN

Andrews McMeel
Publishing, LLC

Kansas City

Also by Jerry Scott and Jim Borgman

Zits: Sketchbook 1
Growth Spurt: Sketchbook 2
Don't Roll Your Eyes at Me, Young Man!: Sketchbook 3
Are We an "Us"?: Sketchbook 4

Treasury

Humongous Zits

Zits® is syndicated internationally by King Features Syndicate, Inc. For information, write King Features Syndicate, Inc., 300 W. 57th, New York, New York 10019.

09 10 MPT 8 7

ISBN-13: 978-0-7407-1854-0
ISBN-10: 0-7407-1854-1

Library of Congress Control Number: 2001090481

Cover design by Tom Borgman

ATTENTION: SCHOOLS AND BUSINESSES

To Beth, Don, Max, Joey, and especially M. J. Wayne.

—J.B.

To Jeff Wambolt. Far out.

—J.S.

9

11

19

26

31

41

51

53

65

66

71

76

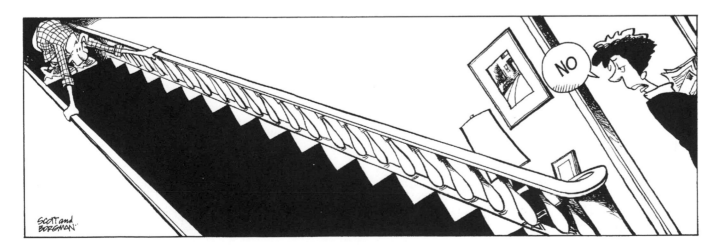

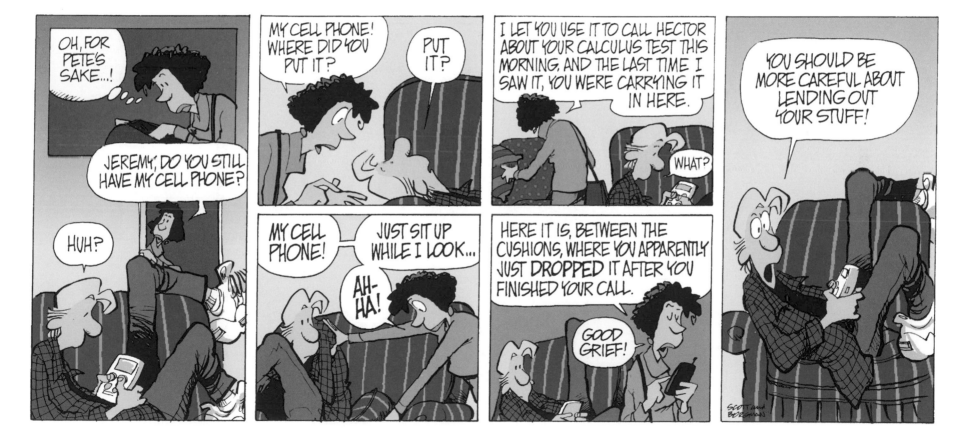

85

94

97

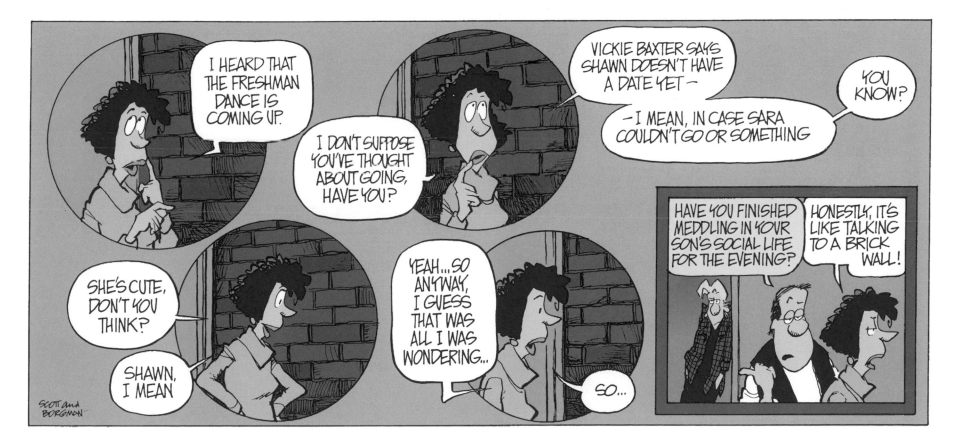

113

Jeremy

You are, unfortunately, fifteen years old.
A high school freshman with, thank God, four good
friends but other than that a seriously boring
life in a seriously boring town made livable only
by the knowledge that someday in the far-off
future at least this will all be over and you'll
turn sixteen and get a driver's license which you
so richly deserve and then life will finally be
good. Oh, and your parents are seriously ruining
your life.

GLUGG GLUG GLUG!

YOU'VE GOT MAIL!

GAAAA!

School sucks. Sometimes it's cool. Grades have been good. Better than good in some cases, without making it a religion. Definitely you'll go to college, you guess. Hopefully one with a beach. Music is what you live for, and someday you'll be a rock god who writes his own music and lyrics, unlike these cookie-cutter bands they stamp out these days who couldn't come up with an original sound or verse or play a chord on a guitar if their lives depended on it and whose only talent is synchronized dancing, which does not *even* deserve commentary at this point because you don't want to get into that right now.

Hector Garcia

Jeremy has been your best friend since the fourth grade when you moved here. You guys are amigos and hardly ever get on each other's nerves much, and even when you do it's no big deal because there's way too much history between you to sweat the small stuff. Like the van for example, which, okay, may not be much to look at now, but once you and Jeremy get finished restoring it, is going to be a total love rocket. The plan is to drive across the country starting on the day you get your driver's licenses (parental permission pending) and you won't stop until you hit an ocean. You are so ready for this and your mom and dad are so not going to let you go, but the important thing is to get the stupid thing running and hope for the best even though, as your grandmother says, *"La esperanza es la negación de la realidad"* (Hope is the denial of reality). Whatever.

Sara Toomey

First of all, let's get this boyfriend/girl-friend thing straight. Jeremy is sweet and everything and he's the only guy that you've ever actually wanted to shave your legs for, but the term "girlfriend" just makes your teeth grind because, let's face it, it practically connotes ownership. Besides, you can't name one relationship you've seen that truly works on the basis of total equality or that has the shelf life of, say, a ripe banana. As Dorothy Parker wrote,

"Oh, life is a glorious cycle of song,
A medley of extemporanea;
    And love is a thing that can never go wrong;
And I am Marie of Roumania."

SLAM!

Walt

(prolonged sigh) The boy is, quite honestly, a handful at times. Your first son, Chad, was a piece of cake to parent ... smart, handsome, confident, likable, polite, motivated ... shoot! He could have been raised by dachshunds and turned out okay.

Now Jeremy (that idea of Connie's to name the boys Chad and Jeremy after her favorite '60s rock duo seems dumber every year) is a little different story. The boy seems to brood a lot. That concerns you, but, hey, hormones can explain a lot of odd behavior. Nobody would know that better than an orthodontist who, by profession, is sentenced to spending nearly eight hours of every day staring directly into the jaws of puberty. It's weird. You pride yourself on your ability to listen to and communicate with patients, but when it comes to your own son, you practically have to pry every syllable out of him.

Connie

You're forty-three, probably look it in the jowls, you touch up the gray occasionally, but you are a reasonably fit person with a good marriage and a healthy family. The decision to be a stay-at-home mom until the boys are both in college hasn't been an easy one to live with, but it's paying off. Both Chad and Jeremy (why you ever agreed to Walt's idea of naming them after that stupid singing duo you'll never know) are great kids on their way to becoming great adults.

You have finally found the time to start scratching that creative itch you've had for the last ten years, and it's going surprisingly well! After sixteen short months, you're already three-quarters of the way through chapter one (although it badly needs a rewrite), and it would be further along if Jeremy would just get it through his thick head that the sign you hang on the spare bedroom door says "Do Not Disturb," and not "Please Interrupt Me with an Inane Question or a Request to Drive You Someplace That You Could Easily Have Walked to By Now."

The Band

Goat Cheese Pizza, Chickenfist, Jughead's Hat, and Angry Dwarfs. Nobody can agree on a name, so you're known by all four of these names at various times. Presently consisting of Jeremy (lead guitar/vocals), Hector (rhythm guitar/vocals), Tim (bass guitar/vocals), and Pierce (drums/vocals), the sound is really actually not all that terrible. A little heavy on the vocals, perhaps.

Jeremy

Founding member, lead guitarist, lead vocals, and spiritual guide for the band. Writes most of the songs, schedules rehearsals, lugs amps, and creates buzz.

Hector

Rhythm guitarist and the glue that holds the group together. Acts as the voice of reason during times of dispute, which, when totaled, exceeds the time spent playing music by almost half.

Tim

Took up the bass for two reasons: 1) Cool sound, and 2) Had four strings instead of six and looked easier to play than a regular guitar.

Y.A.

The original drummer for the band. Quit the band for personal reasons (thought it sucked).

Pierce

Brought in to replace Y.A. Has everything a garage band drummer should have ... danger, mystery, energy, and partially deaf parents. Doesn't suffer fools gladly and wears a constant scowl ... understandable for someone with three pounds of jewelry on his head.

Chad

Things come easy for you. There. It's said. It's not fair, but hey, you never asked for the 157 I.Q. or the athletic body or the thick hair or the square jaw or any of it. It's just who you are, okay? Sometimes it feels like your sole purpose in life is to act as a beacon that shines on the inadequacies of your poor little doofus of a brother. Jeremy is pretty bright and funny and not a bad guitar player, but he has to go through high school constantly in the shadow of his **valedictorian/All-American/cheerleader-dating/homecoming king** of a big brother. You are haunted by this injustice and often discuss it openly with others. Your pain is eased only by the fact that women find this **vulnerability irresistible.**

Brittany

You are, quite simply, the information pipeline for the freshman class. The server, the router, the hub--whatever. You know stuff, okay? All rumors in this school either pass through or originate with you. People have come to count on you for this, as well as for freelance opinions on fashion, romance, etiquette, and, of course, relationship counseling. But possibly your greatest gift is critiquing others. Through an incredibly fortunate combination of an acute sense of cool and good old-fashioned chutzpah, you possess the ability to immediately point out the shortcomings of others, sometimes even before they occur. It's like a seventh sense or something, and because it's so rare and specialized, not everyone can appreciate the favor that you're doing them when your wisdom is shared. Their loss.

The Posse

Ohmigawd! You are so the best friends in the world and you do *not* know what you would do without each other's friendship and support and lip gloss because it's a harsh world out there and it is not easy to get along on one's own which is why you choose to roam as a pack. Zuma, Redondo, and LaJolla ... the three of you have been best-best friends forever, share the same taste in fashion as well as smoothies, finish each other's sentences, and have logged more sleepover hours than a cross-country flight attendant.

RichandAmy

Every high school has one. You are the couple that fell in love early and never got out. Deeply. Madly. Sincerely. Nauseatingly. Against all odds (and some laws of physics), you have devised enough methods of maintaining skin contact with one another in an academic environment to fill an encyclopedia. In fact, your names even touch. Sure, people stare and everything, but that's just because they're jealous that you found your true soul mate before they did, the poor lost lambs.

FRESHMAN PROM

The Van

A 1962 VW Split-Window Kombi (Chassis no. 930236 Engine no. HO514881). You are the Holy Grail of classic Volkswagen vans, at least as far as some people are concerned. After you spent the past seventeen years rusting away to scrap behind some hippie farmer's barn, Jeremy and Hector found you and have elevated your status considerably. With elaborate and colorful plans having been made for your complete restoration, you are now rusting away to scrap behind Jeremy's garage.

Maybe that's too harsh. They actually do try to work on you from time to time, and have made some progress ... at least your radio works now. The odds that they'll ever get you up and running again are at least fifty to one, but, as in most things in life, it's the journey, not the destination that counts. For now, being the place where dreams are dreamed and plans are planned and teenage boys imagine themselves as Jack Kerouacs is a pretty good place to be. At least it beats having chickens roosting in your engine compartment.

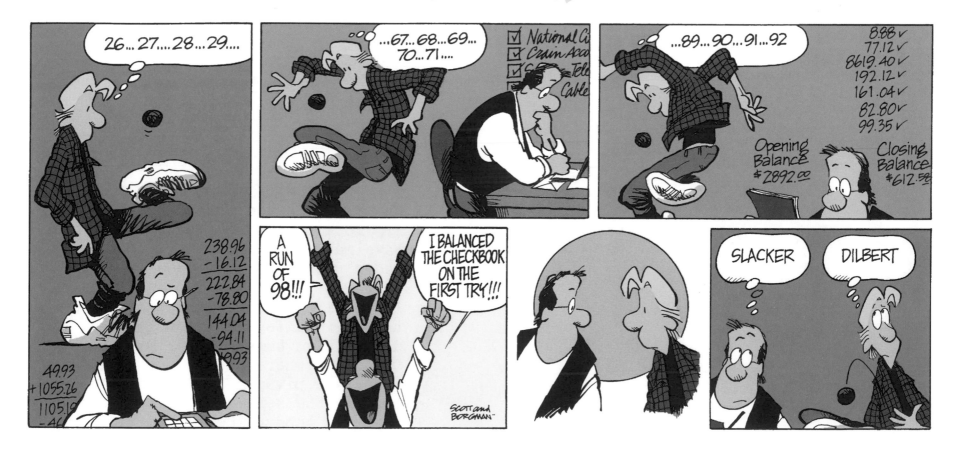

141

146

151

153

Zits
by Jerry Scott and Jim Borgman

158

159

160

163

165

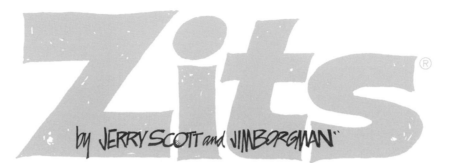

Zits

by JERRY SCOTT and JIM BORGMAN

169

179

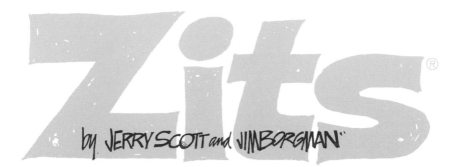

182

186

189

190

191

195

201

202

215

218

225

229

231

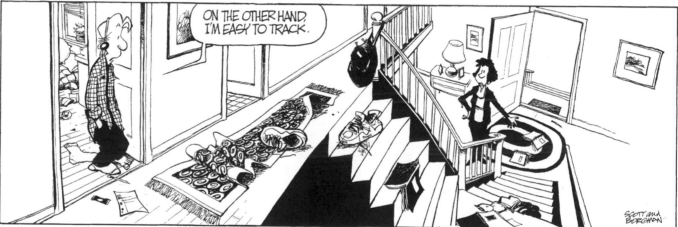

244